The game of basketball has been everything to me. My place of refuge, place I've always gone where I needed comfort and peace. It's been the site of intense pain and the most intense feelings of joy and satisfaction. It's a relationship that has evolved over time, given me the greatest respect and love for the game.

Michael Jordan

A basketball team is like the five fingers on your hand. If you can get them all together, you have a fist. That's how I want you to play.

Mike Krzyzewski

Allah says in the Qur'an not to despise one another. So the criterion in Islam is not color or social status. It's who is most righteous. If I go to a mosque - and I'm a basketball player with money and prestige - if I go to a mosque and see an imam, I feel inferior. He's better than me. It's about knowledge.

Hakeem Olajuwon

I treated it like every day was my last day with a basketball.

LeBron James

March is a month without mercy for rabid basketball fans. There is no such thing as a 'gentleman gambler' when the Big Dance rolls around. All sheep will be fleeced, all fools will be punished severely... There are no Rules when the deal goes down in the final weeks of March. Even your good friends will turn into monsters.

Hunter S. Thompson

It's a heavy duty to try to do everything and please everybody. My job was to go out there and play the game of basketball as best I can and provide entertainment for everyone who wanted to watch basketball. Obviously, people may not agree with that; again, I can't live with what everyone's impression of what I should or what I shouldn't do.

Michael Jordan

Everyone needs a coach. It doesn't matter whether you're a basketball player, a tennis player, a gymnast or a bridge player.

Bill Gates

What you are as a person is far more important than what

you are as a basketball player.

John Wooden

I don't know what I'm going to do tomorrow. I just know for sure I'm going to keep playing basketball.

Kevin Durant

Baseball is a team game but, at the same time, it's a very lonely game: unlike in soccer or basketball, where players roam around, in baseball everyone has their little plot of the field to tend. When the action comes to you, the spotlight is on you but no one can help you.

Chad Harbach

There is no such thing as a perfect basketball player, and I don't believe there is only one greatest player either.

Michael Jordan

I'm a basketball player. That's what I do and what I love but that's just not all who I am. I'm talented in a lot of different areas.

Kevin Durant

I have to tell you, I'm proudest of my life off the court. There will always be great basketball players who bounce that little round ball, but my proudest moments are affecting people's lives, effecting change, being a role model in the community.

Magic Johnson

When I was young, I had to learn the fundamentals of basketball. You can have all the physical ability in the world, but you still have to know the fundamentals.

Michael Jordan

The invention of basketball was not an accident. It was developed to meet a need. Those boys simply would not play 'Drop the Handkerchief.'

James Naismith

I want people to follow their dreams, yes... but I'm not interested in telling young black kids how to be rappers... I want to show them that there's so many other paths you can take, besides a rapper or basketball player.

J. Cole

February is always a bad month for TV sports. Football is gone, basketball is plodding along in the annual midseason doldrums, and baseball is not even mentioned.

Hunter S. Thompson

My greatest gift that I have in life is basketball.

Isaiah Thomas

Hockey is a sport for white men. Basketball is a sport for black men. Golf is a sport for white men dressed like black pimps.

Tiger Woods

My personal life is the same. At the end of the day, this is just a job. I love what I do, and it's a great job. But it's like my alter ego. There's Chris Brown the singer. And there's Christopher Brown, the down-home Tappahannock boy that plays video games and basketball and hangs out.

Chris Brown

Michael Jordon may have been the best basketball player in

history, but he couldn't have won six NBA titles without a team.

Mark E. Hyman

Basketball is a team game. But that doesn't mean all five players should have the same amount of shots.

Dean Smith

There's a tipping point that happens with soccer in which you just kinda get it. I was drawn to it because the best soccer teams play similarly to my favorite basketball teams - like the eighties Lakers or eighties Celtics - teams that emphasized teamwork over individualism and relied on passing as their biggest ongoing edge.

Bill Simmons

I'm not a role model... Just because I dunk a basketball doesn't mean I should raise your kids.

Charles Barkley

I don't know how tall I am or how much I weigh. Because I don't want anybody to know my identity. I'm like a superhero. Call me Basketball Man.

LeBron James

Drama is played at the pace of chess... or billiards... or poker. Engrossing? Sure. But comedy is played at the jubilant, high-octane speed of sports like basketball or hockey.

Mark Waters

I had an extremely boring time doing 20 to 30 trades a day while everyone was talking about baseball or basketball. So I stood there fantasizing about a device that could do the same thing I was doing.

Thomas Peterffy

It's hard to play basketball when nothing is inside of you.

Ben McLemore

I grew up believing that one person could make a difference. In Indiana, you saw that with basketball. The small town could beat the big town, like in the movie 'Hoosiers.' That is one of the things that attracts me to entrepreneurs.

Mary Meeker

Then you've got Georgetown, and I really just like everything about them. When I went down there with my mom, it really opened my eyes to what they were all about. I have to factor in what a school like that can do for me, even away from being a basketball player.

Nerlens Noel

I was a roving guard on the Lowell Hebrew Community Center's girls' basketball team all through high school. My specialty was stealing the ball, but my only shot was a lay-up.

Elinor Lipman

I was never really a model. That somehow is in my bio. The whole thing is I was tall since I was a child - you're either a model or you play basketball.

Jules Asner

I was pretty much seen as a basketball player coming out of

high school. Football was my second love, but luckily, I turned out to be pretty good. Something just drew me to football; besides, I ended up being too short for my position in basketball.

Justin Tuck

I used to play football all the time. In the U.S., people don't play football, so I had to learn basketball. Looking back, that's what I like about my life - doing new things, having a new perspective.

Barkhad Abdi

I wasn't a bad basketball player, but I was far from the world's greatest. Good defense, no offense - that was me.

Chuck Connors

Basketball is what got me out of the projects. It got my momma the house she never had, the car she never had. Nobody is going to get the best of me. You might score more points than me, but you're going to know you were in a dogfight.

Kenyon Martin

I think that basketball players should get the job done no matter how it looks on the screen.

Oscar Robertson

Those companies that don't see the black and brown communities are missing, out of their closed eye, talent, which leads to money and growth. When baseball, football and basketball couldn't see the field, they missed talent and growth. The same is true in the tech industry.

Jesse Jackson

I wanted to do two things when I was growing up, about your age. I wanted to play in the NBA, and I wanted to be a businessman after my basketball career was over, and that is what I am doing now.

Magic Johnson

I've tried to handle winning well, so that maybe we'll win again, but I've also tried to handle failure well. If those serve as good examples for teachers and kids, then I hope that would be a contribution I have made to sport. Not just basketball, but to sport.

Mike Krzyzewski

I was a better basketball player growing up in high school than I was a swimmer. Basketball to this day is my favorite sport.

Ryan Lochte

I either run or try to play basketball every day.

Harold Ford, Jr.

You need a teaching coach who understands the game of basketball, not just some guy coming on the court talking about Xs and Os.

Oscar Robertson

I'm the girl who's like, 'Why wear heels when I can wear tennis shoes and be comfortable?' I've always been the girl who's like, 'Let's go play basketball.'

Kyla Pratt

I feel like I have another level every year that I start a new season of basketball. If I continue to keep growing, and make everything consistent, I'm going to get better and better each year.

Victor Oladipo

We'd wait for my dad to come home from work, and he'd take 15, 20 minutes to just throw a football or shoot basketball hoops or kick a soccer ball or play volleyball. That was always a big part of my childhood, and I know it must have helped me with sitting down and doing homework later or falling asleep. It was a great way to use up some energy.

Andrew Luck

Magic is who I am on the basketball court. Earvin is who I am.

Magic Johnson

OK, I'll put it like this: I doubt if we will see another All-American basketball athlete who is a Rhodes Scholar.

Kareem Abdul-Jabbar

I love basketball.

Floyd Mayweather, Jr.

Basketball was not my main sport in grade school, or even the first year of high school.

Mike Krzyzewski

I had concussions as a kid playing football and basketball, and know what it feels like and to have someone say 'Just rub some dirt on it, and get back in there.'

Billy Corgan

I started out as a football player. I liked to inflict pain. In basketball, it was the same thing.

Shaquille O'Neal

I like playing basketball and going to the gym. I don't box, but I'll ride my bike and go jogging or running in the park. Sometimes my lady and I go hiking.

Kevin Hart

Everyone thought I was going to die like a year later, they didn't know. So I helped educate sports, and then the world, that a man living with HIV can play basketball. He's not going to give it to anybody by playing basketball.

Magic Johnson

When I'm done playing basketball, I want do something bigger. I'm working on my doctorate right now at Barry University in Florida.

Shaquille O'Neal

I think I've gotten more attention after the Olympics than any other U.S. athlete, and it's really great that people are recognizing who I am and what I do. You look at Shaq and you see a basketball player. You look at Tiger Woods and you see a golfer. But people are responding to who I am.

Johnny Weir

Trip Hawkins - and this was the early 1980s - was saying there's going to be a day when everyone has a computer and they're going to want to do more on it, including playing games. So he started up a company, EA Sports, and he was going to have three games, football, basketball and baseball. So I was the football game.

John Madden

Competing in both track and field and basketball for the Bruins I have a lot of great memories to choose from. But my all-time favorite moment in collegiate sports has to be in 1982 when we won UCLA's first NCAA title in track.

Jackie Joyner-Kersee

And my father didn't have money for me to go to college. And at that particular time they didn't have black quarterbacks, and I don't think I could have made it in basketball, because I was only 5' 11". So I just picked baseball.

Willie Mays

The thing I like about my body is that it's strong. I can move furniture around my apartment. I can ride my horse... I can play basketball. It's a well functioning machine.

Cindy Crawford

It's not to hurt anyone, but basketball can be rough.

Sue Wicks

As a child, I was very active. I was a gymnast, I played

touch football, netball and basketball. When I was 16 years old, I started yoga. I started working out at an early age.

Miranda Kerr

Nobody cared about swimming. You could draw a crowd for basketball.

Merlin Olsen

In the tennis world, there weren't a whole lot of Asians playing. You see it a little bit more now. The same can really be said for basketball.

Michael Chang

When I was a kid, I was always an athlete. I played a lot of sports. I played football, basketball, baseball and soccer.

Scott Caan

I sail, scuba dive, play football, basketball.

Casper Van Dien

Millions of guys play millions of basketball games every day of the week at the playground or the YMCA. But LeBron James gets $20 million a year because he can jam on all of those guys. We're always going to want to see LeBron and Kobe go at it.

Adam Carolla

I remember one time being told I could not play in a basketball game at the College of William and Mary because I was black, even though I was playing with a United States Army team.

Walter Dean Myers

If a director brings a guy to their movie who does improv, they've got to let him do what he does - otherwise it's like bringing Michael Jordan to your basketball team and telling him to just pass the ball and don't shoot.

J. B. Smoove

I'm a competitive person. I love the game of basketball. I'm a gym rat.

Paul Pierce

I think I was a good student, because I jumped over a school. My main interest was basically history and literature. Sports were basically basketball and swimming at a pool. I was so happy.

Shimon Peres

I'm not gonna be bad at anything, and I want to actually be the best at anything I'm doing. So if I'm playing basketball, if I'm taking the SATs, like, there's a competitive spirit behind it. With production, it's the same thing.

J. Cole

Then I went to UCLA - so of course I became a huge Bruin basketball fan... and later came to football.

Leigh Steinberg

I was captain of the volleyball team and the basketball team, and I ran track.

Sarah Shahi

One thing my dad always told me, was he would make sure I always had what he didn't have. He couldn't play basketball because he didn't have tennis shoes - so I had five pairs of tennis shoes.

Robert Griffin III

It's easier to date a football player for sure. Football players have one game a week, and they practice every day, but they're all at home. In basketball, they're on the road all the time.

Khloe Kardashian

In the original script, my character was a basketball player rather than a boxer. I didn't think I could pull that off. I'm a little short to be a basketball player!

Eddie Murphy

I live in L.A., so I go to basketball games. But I love baseball.

Penny Marshall

I've got to make some decisions just like any other player that has ever played this game, that eventually the clock stops, their basketball clock stops.

Alonzo Mourning

Basketball has consumed me since the age of 7 or 8. I don't know what I would do without it.

Rick Pitino

Basketball is my passion, and I love it, and I love to see my players succeed. I'm here for them and my children. That's my passion.

Rick Pitino

Trying to take money out of politics is like trying to take jumping out of basketball.

Bill Bradley

It took me a while to realize that basketball wasn't football.

Merlin Olsen

Football, basketball, and the Olympic sports all have their problems with banned substances.

Jim Sensenbrenner

Like basketball, fashion is hard work.

Amar'e Stoudemire

If I would have listened to other people back in 2000 telling me I should have stopped playing basketball because of a kidney disease, I wouldn't have won a world championship.

Alonzo Mourning

I've always been like that. I was a tomboy when I was a kid, so I was always playing baseball and basketball and football and stuff as a kid with the boys.

Catherine Bell

I love fashion as much as I love basketball! It is a great joy for me to express myself through designing my own collection.

Hakeem Olajuwon

The fact is that everybody around a college basketball

game - the coaches, the announcers, even the referees at a lower level - calculates when the game is really over. They calculate it with intuition and guesswork.

Bill James

In a lot of the really impoverished areas of Johannesburg you see these packets of cheesy puffs which are like 6 feet long and the width of a basketball, and they're transparent and they have like 10,000 cheesy puffs in them, and you can buy that for like 50 cents. It's kind of a weird treat that you'd see people having in the townships.

Neill Blomkamp

I played a lot of sports and it's the plays in basketball that weren't worked out that are the ones that are just fantastic that you remember. We don't know the power that's within our own bodies.

Dave Brubeck

As you get older, stuff starts to wear down. I can't play four basketball games a week anymore. It takes me three days to recover from one. I'm a little older, a little scrappier. So now I do yoga instead. And whatever else happens in the day, I'm set up in the best way possible. I feel great. I'm so flexible.

Stephen Lang

Basketball is basketball.

Oscar Robertson

I had never picked up a basketball before. I went through a grueling audition process. It was almost as if I was learning to walk. It would be like teaching somebody to dance ballet for a role.

Sanaa Lathan

We must take down the carnies. I think we need to start a campaign to defeat their scamming ways. I never win the boardwalk basketball game.

Melissa Rauch

I would never do 'Dancing With The Stars,' because it's just not fair. I am too good of a dancer. It would be like LeBron James playing little league basketball.

Terry Crews

Basketball made me happy to be tall. And more secure about myself than I ever would have been without it.

Matt Emmons

Anytime you're playing basketball, and you have a coach who you have to respect, you've got to be very disciplined.

Romeo Miller

Handball, swimming, running, jumping, basketball, and boxing were as much a part of me as breathing.

Gene Tunney

I usually just speak in English when I'm on the basketball court. For some reason, my mind never even tried to cross any other language when I'm playing basketball.

Dikembe Mutombo

I never looked at basketball as work. I always enjoyed it as my hobby. I loved it. Once that love is gone, and I'm tired of working out every day and doing all the stuff to get me ready for games, and I'm tired of lifting and conditioning and doing all that other stuff around it, and I'd rather stay in bed, then it's time to go.

Dirk Nowitzki

I realize that I'm not going to be doing interviews for the cover of 'GQ' for the rest of my life, know what I mean? I'm on TV because I play basketball really well.

Chris Paul

For example, Michael Jordan earns $100million a year but continues to play basketball and remains a modest human being.

Franz Beckenbauer

There are lots of things that I will probably never experience in this life. Military combat. Being dictator of a small central American country. Dunking a basketball. Being a famous rock star. Or walking on Mars. But one thing I have been, and will always be, is an entrepreneur.

Michael Arrington

I play a lot of basketball.

Josh Peck

Tennis was always there for me, which was lucky. I would go play baseball, basketball, football, hang with my brother, do whatever, and at the end of the day I'd come back and say, 'Hey, Mom, would you hit 15 minutes worth of balls with me?'

Jimmy Connors

My focus is on comfort, so I tend to keep it simple and casual - both during and after the basketball season.

Tony Parker

I've written in every imaginable location; a repurposed closet, the kitchen table, the bleachers while my kids had basketball practice, the front seat of the car when they were at soccer. In airports. On trains. In the break room when I was supposed to be wolfing down dinner. In the back of classrooms when I was supposed to be paying attention.

Laurie Halse Anderson

I was a baseball player at North Central High School in Spokane, Washington even though I was all-city in basketball, even when I signed a letter of intent to play quarterback at Washington State.

Ryne Sandberg

Basketball, in America, is like a culture. It is like a foreigner learning a new language. It is difficult to learn foreign languages and it will also be difficult for me to learn the culture for basketball here.

Yao Ming

I love basketball players for what they do for their size - so graceful.

Warren Moon

I'm a huge, huge sports fan, and Marquette basketball is my No. 1 thing.

Danny Pudi

The weird thing about rap is that you don't get compared in the same way that athletes do, even though it's probably the most competitive sport in music. In basketball, they look at a player and say: 'This guy was the best in his prime at this sport.' But in rap it's not until you're dead or retired that people think about it like that.

Chance The Rapper

Involvement in my kids' sports teams is something I have made time for over the years. I've also been able to coach all three of them in baseball and basketball, something that has strengthened our bonds and given me indescribable joy. I wouldn't trade it for anything.

Thomas Perez

I wanted to emulate my parents - Mum captained India in basketball, and Dad won a bronze in hockey in 1972 Olympics. My focus has always been to achieve excellence whether in the field of tennis, in the corporate field, in the art of acting or in motivating youngsters.

Leander Paes

If I had not played basketball and made the millions of dollars that I had made, I would never have been able to build a hospital in Congo. It started in 1997, and 10 years later I was able to unveil the Biamba Marie Mutombo Hospital, named after my mother, in my hometown outside of Kinshasa. It was such a blessing.

Dikembe Mutombo

My own basketball background was ripping up my ACL in a lawyer's league.

David Stern

I love sports. I've played basketball, baseball, soccer, tennis, track and field growing up.

Michael B. Jordan

My dad never really played basketball, but now he's my biggest critic. I come home, and he says: 'Why didn't you shoot there? Why didn't you drive?'

Dirk Nowitzki

All you have to do is drive by the empty tennis courts and basketball courts and compare them to the skate parks... c'mon people, get with the program - the future is now!

Jeff Ament

I think we have our sports within our own culture that are huge with baseball, football, basketball, and hockey. Those are the sports in America that we grow up with and soccer isn't really there yet.

Claudio Reyna

I was born in Chicago, then I spent most of my youth in Joliet, Illinois which is about thirty minutes south, and I went to a military academy for high school in Wisconsin. Then I went to college, on a basketball scholarship to a small school in Iowa, so I'm like Mr. Midwest.

Adam Rapp

I played in Joe Louis in a playoff game. I played there when the roof caved in for half a season. The facility is great for basketball because it goes straight up, so you feel like the fans are on top of you.

Bill Laimbeer

I just want to try to ignore the scrutiny and all the distractions and just play hard basketball and let the best come... Improving game by game and trying to improve my game is what I want to do.

Andrew Bogut

The caliber of play suffered and attendance declined year by year. Interest in college football was exploding, and there was this new game called basketball.

John Thorn

As the wonderful agony begins for 1964-65, I sometimes wonder why I do it. I've got an insurance business going on the side, and it is starting to grow nicely. Selling insurance fulfills me, in a way, like basketball. But basketball keeps calling me back. I suppose I'll play until I can't keep up with the kids any longer.

Tom Heinsohn

No one missed more basketball in the history of NBA than I did. I played 14 seasons, on the roster for 14 years, and I missed more than nine-and-a-half full seasons.

Bill Walton

We can never thank David Stern enough. His vision to use basketball to improve the quality of our lives to make this world a better and saner place, that guy, is the most important man in the history of basketball.

Bill Walton

My first motion capture game was with Sony - 'NBA: The Life.' It was very ahead of its time. Brandon Akiaten, he was the writer and director. He had a real vision of what this game was meant to be; it was a basketball game where I was the Jerry Maguire sports agent type guy. And it was great!

Nolan North

I want the 'Book of Basketball' to do well if only so I can shop an absolutely ridiculous topic for my next book: like, a book about basketball cards, or an unauthorized biography of A. J. Daulerio.

Bill Simmons

When I watch kids play basketball, they don't know how to think the game. They know what it should look like, but they don't know why.

Lisa Leslie

I played baseball, and that's pretty much it. Basketball came late, this was, basketball was the sport that I tried to master, I kind of mastered baseball, so basketball was one of those things where I wanted to master this game, so that's why I probably play it the way I do.

Eric Williams

I'm a Christian first. I'm a family guy second. As much as I like coaching, as much as I like basketball, it's third, fourth, or fifth down the line.

Steve Alford

The hand check has always been a part of pro basketball.

Stu Jackson

I'm really into basketball, baseball, football and working out - but you'll never catch me in a public sauna.

Joey Lawrence

I was very fortunate when I was little - I played basketball. You really absolutely learn how to be a team player, how to win a game, to accomplish things, not just for yourself.

Weili Dai

I loved the glamour and excitement of the games and, in particular, knowing the names of each and every one of the referees - that's because my mom, a former basketball player, would yell at them from our front-row seats for making bad calls!

Hannah Storm

I was always doing something physical. My brothers and I used to have handstand contests. We'd walk around the projects on our hands and see who could get the farthest. I was always playing football with them, basketball or racing in the street.

Florence Griffith Joyner

I enjoy listening to classical music and heavy metal. I play basketball and try to go diving at least once a year. I don't really have hobbies in the traditional sense... I engage in too many activities already through the actions of my characters.

Alan Dean Foster

Coach Wooden, when he speaks, you listen. I've taken a lot of things from him and his little blue book because to him, it's not just about basketball, it's about life as well.

Kevin Love

Sitting behind the bench at games is the hardest thing I've ever had to go through because basketball is really most of my happiness. So when I can't go out there and exert energy and have fun and things like that, it kind of puts everything else into perspective.

Chris Webber

Basketball's eras are defined by teams - Celtics, Lakers, Bulls - and baseball's epochs are defined by players - Ruth, Robinson, Mantle - but with football, it's the sideline strategists, the nutty professors and top coated Lears.

J. R. Moehringer

The only reason I went to college was to play basketball. I injured my knee and couldn't play.

Jeffrey Dean Morgan

The basketball coach cut me within two days, so I was back in the pool. I was the first one in the wall after the first 25 yards, but the last one out because I didn't have a flip turn.

Merlin Olsen

If you're getting ready to do a really emotional scene then, right before it, you're probably not going to be outside playing basketball.

Emilie de Ravin

I tried to make a point of doing things outside the box, of not having basketball consume me.

Grant Hill

Pro basketball is a very mercenary endeavor.

Rick Majerus

Baseball is like cricket, and I grew up in a country where they had cricket. So I understand cricket, soccer and basketball. I played basketball at the club level and a little bit in college, so that's why I'm a basketball fanatic.

Patrick Soon-Shiong

I worked every day - Christmas Eve, birthdays - trying to become a great basketball player. Everywhere I went, I had a basketball.

Harvey Mason, Jr.

Throughout my journey in basketball, I always have someone to talk to in my father. I know how hard he had to work as an athlete.

Joakim Noah

I run in the morning, lift weights in the afternoon, basketball training at night, and then lift weights again at night.

Lil' Romeo

We're talking about being relevant again. I want the Sixers to be on people's tongues again... I want the Sixers to be the basketball team that people want to see.

Doug Collins

A lot of people talk about the Fab Five, and they were wonderful, one of the best teams you'll ever see in college basketball. But the '89 team is the best one to ever play at Michigan in my opinion because they won the national championship. Winning a championship is winning a championship.

Trey Burke

About the time you think you are getting to know the
moves in this game, someone comes along and does
everything but undress you on the basketball floor.
Standing there under the basket with your hands cupped -
and finding that you don't have the ball in them - is a great
little old leveler.

Tom Heinsohn

In every game, there's three teams out there. There's the
two basketball teams and the team of officials. If the two
teams are evenly matched, it can come down to number of
possessions. If one out-of-bounds call goes the wrong way,
that can be the difference.

Tom Heinsohn

Both of us played basketball, and I played tennis and my
knees are done. Now if you ask us head-to-head who wins
at golf, I'm asking for a couple of strokes.

Michael Wilbon

When I was growing up, we used to play basketball in a

park that was never shoveled when it snowed. The basketball rims were never fixed. And we understood then that there was a relationship between public policy and our quality of life.

DeForest Soaries

I love sports. When I'm not playing, I'm watching, reading, or otherwise obsessing about them. This probably stems from growing up in Indiana, where if you didn't at least attempt to play basketball, you were considered of dubious moral character.

Mark Waters

I think the greatest all-around athlete ever was Jim Brown. He played lacrosse, basketball and ran track at Syracuse. He played professional football for the Browns.

Will McDonough

Yugoslavia was a kind of superpower. Great movies. Beautiful novels. Great rock-and-roll. We became a superpower in basketball. The problem is that people needed to identify more strongly with it after Tito and his awful, tricky way of leading the country.

Emir Kusturica

Seven years ago, my father and I realized that our relationship was extremely unique, especially in the African-American community. He raised me to not only understand the fundamentals of basketball and to try to be a player with a high basketball IQ, but he wanted me to understand that my image and my name meant more than stats.

Allan Houston

My teammates at Duke - all of them, black and white - were a band of brothers who came together to play at the highest level for the best coach in basketball.

Grant Hill

The accomplishments in college and even in the pros are more in my mind because you constantly see Duke on TV during basketball season. You constantly see the NBA.

Grant Hill

I played basketball to try to get my parents from working so hard.

James Worthy

As all of us with any involvement in sports knows, no two umpires or no two referees have the same strike zone or call the same kind of a basketball game.

Herb Kohl

Basketball was my whole life until I was 20 years old. All I knew was basketball. Then came golf, and I thought that's all I wanted to do then.

Kip Moore

I didn't know anything about acting, I didn't know anything about theater, but I was just an exceptional student at high school. I wanted to play ball; I'm going after a basketball scholarship and be a doctor. I got injured and my marks began to drop.

Louis Gossett, Jr.

I was president of the schools in junior high and high school, got a scholarship to New York University, played a little basketball, and was a celebrity.

Louis Gossett, Jr.

I do something that I don't think anyone else does. I warm up before a game. Baseball and basketball players warm up, so why shouldn't the announcer warm up?

Chick Hearn

Spend time with your family and try to spend time doing things that you enjoy doing other than basketball.

Elena Delle Donne

My first love was basketball.

Stan Smith

I started collecting baseball cards and basketball cards when I was younger. I have a CD collection that turned into a DVD collection, and I have a Jordan shoe collection. And I don't drink, but I have a wine collection. I just started a sweatshirt collection. Every city that I'm in, I buy a sweatshirt. It's just something that I do.

Marques Houston

Basketball for me has always been a matter of rhythm -

what you do bouncing the ball, how you bounce the ball, how you run, how you receive the ball to be in rhythm.

Earl Monroe

I have way too many hobbies. I play guitar, and my buddies and I record music in a studio in my house. I have a couple of vintage Jeeps I'm always working on, fixing up. And I ride horses - I grew up on a horse ranch - and play basketball. I need to cut back on my hobbies so I can work more.

Riley Smith

The courts don't remove children from their home because the child underperformed at school or required extra long walks or a game of basketball in order to blow off the steam all 5-year-olds have. It's because the parents were unfit, not the kids.

Angela Featherstone

For me, basketball kind of mirrors life. It sounds deep, but the sport has transformed my personality and my daily coping mechanisms. It has meant a lot.

Robbie Jones

Basketball would have been the natural sport to play, but it's a little too aggressive for me, so instead I dabbled in volleyball and some good old-fashioned Roller Derby.

Jessica Williams

Anytime you have a Pat Riley running things, calling the shots, you are not going to question things because he has been through it. He knows what it is all about and what it takes to win. All we have to do on our end is play basketball because we know the right calls and the right decisions are going to be made up top.

Udonis Haslem

I have feelings, but not when it comes to basketball. I'm here to win. I'm not here to make friends.

Kenyon Martin

I know the game well. I'm a student of basketball; I know what it takes to win.

Kenyon Martin

Every time I was playing basketball, I felt sick to my stomach. I didn't realize that feeling was having to leave my family - having to leave my sister, who can't even communicate with me when I'm gone.

Elena Delle Donne

I'd rather be a face for happiness and doing things that you have a passion for, rather than faking it and pretending like I'm this face of women's basketball, when I can't stand the sport at all.

Elena Delle Donne

We've got to play better basketball.

Tim Buckley

I grew up in Westlake Villiage, a suburb of L.A. There was a guy there who was a fighter and was like, 'I'll teach you to box.' I started a little bit of boxing, then it crossed over into jiu-jitsu. I was into it for a little while, but then I started doing basketball, baseball, team sports.

Jonathan Lipnicki

Collecting shoes is my biggest hobby. I've got a couple hundred pairs of Nikes and Jordans. I got a lot of hats, too. I like to play basketball, but nothing competition wise.

Chumlee

I've always felt that, you know, the Almighty has a lot of things to do other than help my basketball team.

Bobby Knight

I could've played basketball, but my mind was on baseball. I didn't know what I was in for. In high school it was a matter of talent. No one told you what to do.

Eric Davis

I play fantasy basketball and fantasy football, soccer.

Andy Murray

We don't really watch basketball in Australia.

Iggy Azalea

In my first film, I was a basketball player. Like every good actor, I lied when they asked me if I could play.

David Morse

I have an incredible amount of basketball knowledge, and I think a lot of that is derived from having a Hall of Fame college basketball coach who was very knowledgeable of the game and I had a great high school coach who was also very knowledgeable.

Alonzo Mourning

You don't cut anywhere, don't pick down anywhere, don't double screen, no weak side picking. All these things that should happen in a game of basketball don't happen anymore.

Oscar Robertson

I played a little basketball, but basketball interfered with theater season. That's when we did our term plays and did nutshell versions of Shakespeare for English classes. And, believe me, I got a fair amount of looks from the guys on the team. 'You're in theater but you can play football?'

Dennis Haysbert

I've done a lot of basketball drills, not a whole lot of competitive stuff. I have basically been in the gym everyday working on my game, working on the time off that I've had from the game, just getting myself prepared mentally and physically for the season.

Grant Hill

I played a little basketball. Some football in junior high.

Clint Eastwood

I like basketball, and I've been to three games, which is so much more fun than seeing it on TV, I think.

Heidi Klum

I remember playing a high school basketball game where I didn't eat anything for breakfast. I ate, you know, like a PB and J and some chips for lunch and nothing before the game. I didn't make it through the first quarter. I wish I hadn't have learned that way, but it did leave a lasting impression.

Andrew Luck

My little brothers loved baseball. I'm not as big on that as basketball or football, but I understand the game.

Jurnee Smollett

Where I grew up, the basketball courts were rarely used.

Denis Leary

I love the big, like, basketball sweats... and I only wear vintage T-shirts to bed, because I like the super-thin ones.

Brad Goreski

In 1981, at age 31, I was voted the best player in basketball, and the most valuable player in the league.

Julius Erving

Basketball is my favorite sport, and I'm also a very passionate football fan.

Abhishek Bachchan

On the court, Jason Collins is not a huge basketball star, but he has already claimed his place in civil rights history as the first openly gay athlete to play in one of the four major U.S. sports leagues.

Nancy Gibbs

I tore my ACL playing basketball.

Paul Dano

I really do miss playing basketball. I don't play a lot of pick-up games. But I do like using basketball as a form of cross training.

Jackie Joyner-Kersee

I've got a basketball signed by all the greats from Julius Irving to Oscar Robinson. It was at an All Star game I got them all to sign it. So that ain't going nowhere. I'm going to die with that in my casket.

Ice Cube

My house was filled with music. We had a piano, and my brothers and sisters played instruments. Even though I was around it, I played basketball.

Michael Franti

And from the first time I picked up a basketball at age eight - I had a lot of difficulty when I first picked up a basketball, because I was a scrub - there were things that I liked about it.

Julius Erving

I play basketball on Sundays and I'm a very spiritual guy; I read a lot of Eastern philosophy and I meditate.

Garry Shandling

I enjoy the last quarter of all basketball games.

Sarah Silverman

My mother was a champion high-jumper. My three brothers are basketball players. We've all been very athletic.

Grace Jones

I love basketball.

Brandy Norwood

When I come home, it's about my kid, who needs to eat, needs to do homework, and needs to get to basketball. I don't have a lot of time to think about me.

Taraji P. Henson

Basketball and ping-pong are my two forms of exercise.

Kim Gordon

I really want to start playing basketball. I actually bought a new basketball.

Kim Gordon

I played basketball in high school, and I love watching sports - I'll watch everything except maybe hockey.

Andy Roddick

The business always gets in the way of basketball.

Jason Kidd

I play basketball, I surf and swim and go to the cinema and listen to music and read. I like shopping.

Saoirse Ronan

He knew I enjoyed the relationships of college basketball. All along, he was the wise one.

Rick Pitino

My homies that are around me never give me that 'star pass.' I've hung out with some stars who are playing basketball and everyone let's them score all the baskets. Shooting pool, they let them make all the shots. My homies don't let me get away with that.

Jamie Foxx

There are only so many hours you can sit on the bus and watch TV or play basketball or whatever we do to pass the time before we go out onstage.

Kenny Chesney

Kids who I grew up with, who I played ball with, basketball, baseball, and went to parties with - for whatever reason - they ended up in a fundamentally different place than I did. I'm the attorney general of the United States and they are ex-felons.

Eric Holder

If architecture is, as is sometimes said, music set in concrete, then football and basketball may be said to be creativity embodied in team sports.

Michael Mandelbaum

When I first started playing golf, I was heavily into softball and basketball.

Paula Creamer

By delivering a wide array of programming to YouTube, the NBA will be able to connect with its existing worldwide fan base and reach a vast new audience that is passionate about basketball.

Chad Hurley

Mostly I play sports games - football and basketball. 'Inside Drive' and 'NFL Fever.'

Paul Pierce

Theaters are great. They're designed to sound good, not for basketball.

Les Claypool

I could maybe coach kids' basketball. I know enough about basketball where I feel like I could coach 12-year-olds pretty effectively.

Hannibal Buress

I was pretty hot-tempered all through school. I remember my high school basketball coach telling me: 'Boy, if you don't learn to control that temper, you're gonna kill somebody.'

Tony Dorsett

Magic Johnson was in the seventh year of his Hall of Fame career when thoughts of his basketball afterlife led him to the office of uber-executive Michael Ovitz, co-founder of

Creative Artists Agency, Hollywood's most powerful agency.

Don Yaeger

Basketball, man: it is a land of giants.

Amar'e Stoudemire

My father used to always give me a basketball, a skate board, and a bike every Christmas. That's all I wanted every year.

Amar'e Stoudemire

There're a lot of rules to basketball.

Amar'e Stoudemire

I probably follow all sports a little bit. I like hockey quite a bit. I like football. I like college basketball when it gets down to March Madness. I like baseball. I enjoy them all. I watch them all.

Vince Vaughn

I am a basketball junkie, and as a product of the great basketball state of Kansas, I have watched many a ball game between the University of Kansas Jayhawks and the Tar Heels.

Sheri L. Dew

I had never made any plans beyond basketball.

Sheryl Swoopes

I never thought a basketball shoe would be named after a woman, let alone me.

Sheryl Swoopes

Basketball is always a piece of my life, but never the centerpiece.

Rebecca Lobo

Chick Hearn was my favorite broadcaster ever - he's the one who taught me to think basketball, how to love basketball.

Bill Walton

Back in East St. Louis, tennis wasn't the real thing. If you weren't playing baseball, basketball, football, you were kind of on the outside.

Jimmy Connors

When I said I retired from basketball playing, I have retired. You will not see me play again. That is a promise.

Karl Malone

I want my son to never know the mommy who would rather watch him play basketball than play with him.

Marissa Jaret Winokur

I grew up with baseball; I played in Little League and went to games with my dad. But I, as I grew up, became more of a basketball fanatic than a baseball one.

Jonah Hill

I was a total jock growing up. I went to super-dorky basketball clinics and was handpicked to play on a state team called the Texas Heat.

Erin Wasson

I plan to coach at University of Louisville for as long as I can maintain the passion I have for the game of basketball. I don't want to coach anywhere else. I don't believe in anything else as much as I believe in this university and this state. I want to coach as long as they will have me.

Rick Pitino

Stephen A. Smith is the hardest-working man in sports show business. The ubiquitous basketball pundit appears on ESPN about 10 times a day as a regular on the show 'NBA Fastbreak,' a guest commentator on 'Sports Center,' and a pundit on 'ESPNEWS.'

Stephen Rodrick

I'm not going to lie. I check the iTunes charts. It's all about the iTunes charts. I only go on the Internet for the iTunes charts and basketball blogs.

Nate Ruess

Not only is Rip Hamilton an outstanding basketball player, he is also known for giving back to his community.

Jim Gerlach

Not every kid plays football, basketball. Running can be a source to vent and let things out.

J. R. Martinez

I was a sports nut. I stayed after school probably three hours every day - from fall, to winter, to spring. I went from football to basketball to track, and it started all over again. I loved all of it. I just loved being an athlete and all that it entailed. It really accounts for who I am today and even how I think today.

Terry Crews

When I was playing college basketball, I had to work out every day; it benefited me physically.

Romeo Miller

I gravitate toward the team thing. I'm not a golfer - I much prefer basketball.

Michael Eisner

If there wasn't any business and it was just strictly basketball, then there would be no issue, it would probably be done by now. But the team has to protect.

Jason Kidd

The 76ers currently play very good basketball, and we don't. However, we are still only one win behind them. If we continue to improve, we should be on the top of our division at the end of the regular season.

Jason Kidd

My good friend Yao Ming was the first big player in the NBA to come from China. He gave himself to the game and was successful. That inspired the NBA to invest more and do more for the game of basketball. We're building academies not just in China, but in India, Africa, Europe and South America as well.

Dikembe Mutombo

When I travel around the globe, I try as hard as I can to represent the NBA and the game of basketball to the best of my abilities. I get to go around the world and not only share the game but also my philanthropic work. Building a hospital in the Congo is one of the proudest achievements of my life.

Dikembe Mutombo

I grew up in a small town in Illinois, and my dad was a basketball coach. Thanks to him, I have excellent fundamentals in both basketball and baseball.

Nick Offerman

I had no experience with broadcasting basketball games, so I took a tape recorder and went to a playground where there was a summer league, and I stood up in the top of the stands and I called the game.

Ed Bradley

I love the flow of the game. There's a certain fluidity to basketball. I don't enjoy watching baseball or football in the same way.

Adam Yauch

Growing up, I always thought of Detroit as a basketball town because of the Pistons, but everyone says it's really, at its core, a football town.

Ndamukong Suh

Chris Paul is one of the brightest stars in the National Basketball Association, a must-see player with the New Orleans Hornets whose deft ball skills and eye-popping speed have attracted admirers all over the world.

Don Yaeger

Basketball used to be my top priority.

Derek Fisher

I don't feel like basketball is the only way to make a living.

Derek Fisher

Life for me outweighs the game of basketball.

Derek Fisher

I grew up playing sports, football, basketball, baseball, everything, and acting was such a different environment and different world for me.

Cam Gigandet

I went into umpiring at age 16. I got into officiating because of the fact that I could not stand the referees that worked our basketball games.

Doug Harvey

People who understand basketball definitely appreciate what I bring to the table.

Tyson Chandler

I can shoot a three pointer in basketball, and I can kick a soccer ball.

Christopher Mintz-Plasse

Yoga's hard for me, but I know you can really feel the difference when you do it consistently. I'd rather be playing basketball.

Chris Noth

I had a sketch called 'Fedora Basketball,' which was about basketball players having to wear hats; in addition to scoring points, they have to make sure their fedoras don't fall off.

Hannibal Buress

It wasn't until late high school and early college that I gained enough size and skill to make me welcome on intramural basketball teams.

Paul D. Boyer

I think I have the skills. I'm a great judge of talent. I just know basketball.

Tim Hardaway

I had all the normal interests - I played basketball and I headed the school paper. But I also developed very early a great love for music and literature and the theater.

Carlisle Floyd

I played Little League baseball, but I also played basketball. Basketball was my primary sport. When you play basketball seriously, a lot of times, through the summer season, you continue playing. So that replaced me playing baseball.

Chadwick Boseman

I grew up in Michigan, so I played hockey, football and basketball. I played a little bit of lacrosse, too. My brother played more lacrosse and ran track.

Steven Yeun

When I step on that basketball court, I'm thinking about basketball, I'm thinking about winning - but there's so much that goes into thought about how I'm going to open this game up to others. It's so much more than just basketball.

Carmelo Anthony

It takes a tremendous amount of skill to be a football player. And some of these guys have enough skills to do other sports. Soccer could be one. Basketball could be another. Things where you need incredible hand-eye coordination are always options. I think a football player would be able to adapt to a lot of sports.

Troy Polamalu

In an individual sport, yes, you have to win titles. Baseball's different. But basketball, hockey? One person can control the tempo of a game, can completely alter the momentum of a series. There's a lot of great individual talent.

Kobe Bryant

We can have no progress without change, whether it be basketball or anything else.

John Wooden

Growing up, I looked up to major league baseball players, and now these young women have amazing, incredible women all across the board, from swimming to gymnastics to softball to basketball. It is incredible how far women have come and women in sports have come.

Jennie Finch

I am sure that no man can derive more pleasure from money or power than I do from seeing a pair of basketball goals in some out of the way place.

James Naismith

Something I like to do a lot is just sit by water when there's a current and just stare into the water. I don't fish, I don't hunt, I don't scuba, I don't spear, don't boat, don't play basketball or football - I excel at staring into space. I'm really good at that.

Iggy Pop

If you're a basketball player, you've got to shoot.

Oscar Robertson

I think the most important thing about coaching is that you have to have a sense of confidence about what you're doing. You have to be a salesman, and you have to get your players, particularly your leaders, to believe in what you're trying to accomplish on the basketball floor.

Phil Jackson

A lot of late nights in the gym, a lot of early mornings, especially when your friends are going out, you're going to the gym, those are the sacrifices that you have to make if you want to be an NBA basketball player.

Jason Kidd

My days shouldn't be hard because I'm doing what I'm doing and that's playing basketball.

Derrick Rose

You don't play against opponents, you play against the game of basketball.

Bobby Knight

I like low-maintenance girls, but at the same time, classy. She needs to take care of herself. But also be a girl who isn't afraid to get sweaty and play basketball, so it's cool if she's a tomboy.

Chris Brown

Basketball is my passion, I love it. But my family and friends mean everything to me. That's what's important. I need my phone so I can keep in contact with them at all times.

LeBron James

Growing up, I looked up to major league baseball players, and now these young women have amazing, incredible women all across the board, from swimming to gymnastics to softball to basketball.

Jennie Finch

That's the awesome part. Little girls now have a chance to look up and see women playing soccer, basketball, softball and now hockey - and know they can win a gold medal, too.

Angela Ruggiero

I always wanted to be a basketball player. Nothing more, nothing less.

Dirk Nowitzki

Basketball is in my blood. It is my obligation to try.

Hakeem Olajuwon

Faith, family, academics and then sports was the order of priorities in my family. My parents really stuck to these principles when raising me and my two brothers. As long as we took care of everything, they let us play as much basketball as we wanted.

Jeremy Lin

In college I never realized the opportunities available to a pro athlete. I've been given the chance to meet all kinds of people, to travel and expand my financial capabilities, to get ideas and learn about life, to create a world apart from basketball.

Michael Jordan

Magic is crazy. He is that crazy wild guy on the basketball court that is very intense and very serious. He is the guy who lives and eats and breathes basketball. Magic is a guy who would stand for nothing but winning and really prepared himself as well as he prepared his team. Earvin is the complete opposite.

Magic Johnson

I have always maintained that in basketball the importance of the mental to the physical is about four to one.

Bobby Knight

I enjoy basketball. I enjoy coaching basketball. It's the out-of-season stuff I didn't handle well.

Dean Smith

For a competitive junkie like me, golf is a great solution because it smacks you in the face every time you think you have accomplished something. That to me has taken over a lot of the energy and competitiveness for basketball.

Michael Jordan

We don't do things we aren't good at by nature. I wouldn't play basketball because I'm only 5' 1". Find what you enjoy - whether it's racing, flying a helicopter, being a doctor, or stitching clothes together. Once you've done that, you have the passion you need.

Danica Patrick

I'm just a seasonal guy. Basketball, football, baseball, boxing, golf. Give it to me all the time.

Jerry Ferrara

You want to do Olympics just like you do a pro football game or a basketball game? Be my guest. Watch it all fade away.

Dick Ebersol

I was homecoming queen. I was star of my basketball team.

Marla Maples

People see my body and ask me what I do to work out. I play a lot of basketball, so I'm constantly dribbling and running up the court. I take a basketball with me everywhere I go!

Romeo Miller

I led the state in defensive interceptions my senior year, with seven in nine games. Then I went to Montana to play basketball and found out quickly that my college career wasn't going to work out how I'd envisioned it.

Jeff Ament

Kurt Cobain and Courtney Love talked trash about the fact that I hooped. I once stopped to say 'Hi' before a show, and as I walked away, Courtney yelled, 'Go play basketball with Dave Grohl!'

Jeff Ament

I wake at 5 or 5:30 most mornings, make myself a latte and grab a cookie, write until 10 or 11, go have my favorite meal, 'second breakfast,' or grab coffee with friends, or play basketball. Then, around noon, I begin apologizing via email for the manuscripts I can't get to.

Jess Walter

I played all kinds of sports when I was young: tennis, handball, basketball, some soccer. I focused on basketball when I was 16 or 17 and then came to the U.S. when I was 20.

Dirk Nowitzki

I had a basketball net that my dad had put up outside. I went out there and dribbled all day long. I wanted to play basketball. Then I'd go baseball, and then I'd go to football. I remember playing football in a plowed field. I grew up going from one thing to the next wanting to play something.

Joe Gibbs

I was taught by teachers, and if it's one thing I have it's a basketball mind and I try to pass it on and pay it forward.

Doug Collins

There was the misconception out there that I retired after the 2008 season, but that was never the case. I wasn't done with basketball yet, and I'm still not done.

Sheryl Swoopes

I play basketball for love and money, and they come in interchangeable order, depending on how things are going when you ask the question.

Tom Heinsohn

In America, we have three major sports - baseball, football and basketball. They get the most coverage. Then there's things like golf which mop up most of what is left. But track and field? We are way at the bottom of the totem pole.

Maurice Greene

'Family Ties' was a very successful situation comedy. And, in almost every respect, it functioned on a day to day basis like a well-run, well conditioned basketball team. The show was performed live each week in front of a studio audience on Friday night.

Gary David Goldberg

I have 'the first' attached to my name in a whole lot of different aspects when it comes to the sport of basketball.

Lisa Leslie

Balling is balling; it is all just basketball for me and I'm used to playing both games, so it really does not matter if it is international style, American style; it does not matter at all for me.

Tony Parker

People are much more loose if you are having fun. I had a basketball player who was really soft-spoken, and then we played Connect Four with him, and he really opened up!

Hannah Storm

I have no desire to coach basketball.

Kevin Johnson

Basketball players want contact to get a foul called. Slaps on the wrist and bumps on the shoulder are big time to them, and they don't like that. In football, you get that all the time. The whole mental makeup is different.

Warren Moon

I'm pretty athletic and I play basketball a lot.

Jay Hernandez

I first got into acting when I was 14, coming back from a junior high school basketball game. My mom picked me up and she had been mentioning, prior to that, this community production of 'Godspell', a couple towns over. I was reluctant, at first, and she bribed me with some great dinner that was in that town, neighboring the theater.

Skylar Astin

Well, I work out three to four times a week, in a gym, which - thank God - is right in my building here in New York City. It's in the Reebok building, and it's got every kind of weightlifting equipment you can imagine, spread out over six floors, plus basketball courts and everything else. And because it's right in the building, there's no excuse.

Regis Philbin

My kids have played soccer and baseball and basketball, and the parents who come to games are always saying and doing things that are just wildly inappropriate.

Jeff Garlin

As I get older, I find myself way more into sports. I'm in a basketball league. You maybe know some of the people in it. They're real people, not fake ones like me.

Bryan Greenberg

I got on the scale and I weighed around 203. I'm only 5'7. I was about to turn 30, and I wasn't active anymore. So I started working with a nutritionist and a trainer. I played basketball twice a week. And soon it all just became a habit for me. I became addicted to something good for a change.

Jerry Ferrara

I'm truly passionate about basketball. I'm not as passionate about baseball as I am about basketball, but I watch baseball and I watch football. I love sports in general.

Patrick Soon-Shiong

I'm a big sports guy - golf, tennis, baseball, basketball, snowboarding - and I love games.

Jason Dohring

As I look back on the day I signed my professional contract in 1973, I've never gone to sleep wondering if I could pay the bills or take care of my family. That's what basketball has done for me. It's given me the greatest of thrills from high school to college to the Olympics to coaching to broadcasting.

Doug Collins

Sports were a big part of my life. I was the captain of the basketball team in high school, and captain of the basketball team at Princeton.

John W. Rogers, Jr.

I really focused on three things in high school - my company, basketball and my school work.

Ben Casnocha

The biggest scandal I was ever involved in was - in high school, at a basketball game, I shot and scored for the other team.

Darby Stanchfield

If you want to make films, you'll watch Kurosawa. If you want to play a violin, you listen to Seghetti. Same with somebody who has the ambition to play in the NBA. I watch a basketball game; I enjoy it. Somebody who really wants to learn to play is studying whatever is most magnificent that's going on out there.

Robert Pinsky

I'm one of those people who can't watch themselves do anything. I could never watch myself wrestle. I've probably watched a handful of my matches. I never could watch myself. Even when I played college basketball, I hated film days... 'Oh God, I'm gonna watch myself screw up.' I'm just one of those people who can't watch their work.

Kevin Nash

I have always viewed thinking about arguing, about questioning, pushing back with, joking, about sharing and discovering the world and the news as enjoyable, the same way that I view watching basketball.

Chris Hayes

There's discussion in athletics about how sport - where they say 'SportsCenter' has ruined the fundamentals of basketball because it's - it only applauds dunks and three point shots and blocks, and I think, you know, the cable news has done the same thing for politics.

Dan Pfeiffer

I never really called people out. It was more along the lines of teasing a person. It started for me in fifth grade on the basketball court.

Keyshawn Johnson

Only a handful of professional football athletes have had a signature shoe, unlike in basketball where there have been a number of guys.

Keyshawn Johnson

I remember girls watching it in high school, and I thought

the basketball part of the show was cool. And lo and behold, a few years later, I found myself in 'Tree Hill' land.

Stephen Colletti

I started playing baseball and soccer. Those were my sports on the streets and in school when I was growing up. I didn't even start playing basketball until I was 14.

Earl Monroe

I'm a big sports fan - mainly basketball.

Lamorne Morris

I'm not super social, don't really go to parties, or basketball games, or football games very often, the big social occasions.

Taylor Phinney

I'm a huge LeBron James fan. I love The Heat. He's an incredible basketball player.

Ashley Bell

I was about 14, and my friend's stepdad asked me to do a 10K with him because his son - who was more into basketball - didn't want to. It was amazing, and I still remember the time I got: 48:23.

Sean Astin

I played basketball. I went to school and played basketball and was trying to pursue that as a career path and kind of just fell into acting.

Robbie Jones

It's very warm there, so we were outdoors all the time. The local people had programs for us year-round, where as kids we had the opportunity to play football, basketball, baseball, track and field - we just went from one sport to the next, year-round.

Rafer Johnson

Frankie Muniz is amazing at everything he does. Many people don't know that he can play the piano like you wouldn't believe, and he can bowl and play basketball like you wouldn't believe.

Samaire Armstrong

I would love to have a conversation with you when we're working, and if I'm at a basketball game, I'll probably talk to everyone there. That's different. But on the outside world, if I don't know you and you don't know me, I probably cannot sit there and have a conversation.

Emily Rios

Basketball is big stuff in New York. If you're good in it, everybody respects you. Nobody would want to ruin your shooting eye or your shooting arm.

Bob Beamon

When I was coming up in high school, if you wanted to be in the musical it was during the winter, so I had to choose between playing basketball or being in the musical. And I ended up playing basketball.

Ben Schwartz

I'm a Texan. Some of me is still nestled up there in the Catskill Mountains: the summers I spent with my grandfather on the farm and the guys I played basketball with in high school. But then that was it.

Jerry Jeff Walker

To see a player dunk in women's college basketball is just amazing. It's great to see that the game has reached that level now.

Holly Johnson

I was an athlete growing up. I did a lot of sports: soccer, basketball, so I was always so used to hardcore training, a lot of running. I got to a point where I felt like I just wanted to get toned; I didn't need to shed pounds, so now I do Pilates.

Jacquelyn Jablonski

Dinner, basketball game, four guys - classic.

Billy Bush

I started taekwondo at 5 or 6 years old and did a bunch of kick-boxing later, too. Eventually I became a black belt and coached as well. I did some basketball and softball growing up, but most of my activity was martial arts.

JWoww

I kind of wanna be pro basketball, pro skateboarder.

Jackson Brundage

I played varsity on all of them for four years. I'm 5'9 and that's not that tall for a center so I was a forward. I loved playing volleyball and basketball and track I was good at, but it stressed me out.

Bridgette Wilson

I sing the 'Star Spangled Banner,' so I can get into football, basketball and baseball games for free.

John Cullum

I started playing basketball when I was about three years old. After that, everything else just came naturally. I had older cousins that used to let me hang with them, so I got my toughness from them.

Brandon Jennings

I did volleyball, basketball, and track all through high school. And then I went to junior college and I stuck with track because I was good at shot put and discus. And then I got a full ride to Fresno State for their track program. Shot put was my main thing. I was the five-time All-American, and I set a couple records.

Dot Jones

Once you begin reviewing judgment calls, which in basketball there are many, you put yourself on a very slippery slope in terms of what could be reviewed, and ultimately the number of reviews that could take place that would make it unwieldy.

Stu Jackson

I definitely like to stay active. I'm a huge fan of the NBA and the sport of basketball. I love to play pick-up games in Brooklyn where I live.

Brendan Dooling

Once I grew from 6'1' to about 6'6', by that time I was going into 12th grade, and that's when I started wanting to play basketball, because, pretty much basketball players always got the girl.

Eric Williams

My thing is, I want to play basketball, I would enjoy playing in the D-League, but at the same time I don't want to take an opportunity away from a young guy to get exposure. I'm still thinking about it.

Michael Finley

I played football; I was a running back, and I took a hit, and I had a hairline fracture in my leg which no one spotted, and I was playing basketball all winter and it got worse. And then I was long jumping, about 20 feet, and I landed one time and there was this big crack, and all the bones were jutting out of my leg.

Nick McDonell

Someone once accused me of slumming. I don't know what that means. I play basketball. And through that, I get to see a world that is not smart-kid world.

Nick McDonell

Since I left basketball, and my wife, it's been a glorious feast of lovemaking.

Rick Fox

My dad was my coach in baseball and early on in basketball, so playing baseball was something we always did.

Matthew Stafford

The game of basketball is not played with throwing punches, throwing elbows.

Mo Williams

I went to an ACC school, Wake Forest, I'm a big college basketball fan, and it was just a natural interest for me.

Lee Norris

I sort of tried to get a basketball scholarship out of high school, but that didn't happen. Then I started working for UPS, and that paid for tuition for school. I moved to a bigger town, Louisville. I did it for a year. I had to work the graveyard shift. And then you get off at eight for classes, so that sucked. Then I dropped out.

Boyd Holbrook

When I got into high school, I got really into basketball. I had this itch that I wanted to just move. I didn't know what I wanted to do, but I knew that if basketball became a scholarship or something, it would be a means to that. It turned out I couldn't jump that high.

Boyd Holbrook

I watch a lot of NBA basketball, especially with the playoffs.

Coby Bell

I remember wearing the big oversized baseball and basketball jerseys and Timbaland boots. I was a tomboy growing up. I recently caught a picture of myself, and I was like, 'God! What was I thinking about?'

Drew Sidora

I don't think people can watch University of Texas basketball or football games with me - really, anything Texas is playing - without wanting to punch me in the face. I'm as big a Longhorn fan as you'll find.

Jordan Spieth

Nature, God, Buddha - someone has given me this health. I can break dance still; I can run; I can play basketball. In my mind, I can do anything. As long as I have that spirit, I'm going to keep doing it.

James Hong

One of the questions I get asked a lot is, 'What do you do to stay in shape?' My glib answer is, 'I play.' But I mean it. Sure, I go to the gym, but I don't spend my life there. Most of my activity is outdoors, whether it's basketball or mountain biking or rock climbing.

Jason Lewis

Baseball happens to be a game of cumulative tension but football, basketball and hockey are played with hand grenades and machine guns.

John Leonard

My parents were kind of over protective people. Me and my sister had to play in the backyard all the time. They bought us bikes for Christmas but wouldn't let us ride in the street, we had to ride in the backyard. Another Christmas, my dad got me a basketball hoop and put it in the middle of the lawn! You can't dribble on grass.

Jimmy Fallon

As long as you put on a jersey, no matter what kind of jersey it is, as long as you're supporting the game of basketball, I enjoy it.

Dwyane Wade

I'm not going to lie; listen, I'm nice at basketball.

Drake

You know, God gave me a gift to do other things besides play the game of basketball.

LeBron James

I'm not playing for other people; if I start thinking in those terms I would put too much pressure on myself. I play basketball because that is what I love to do.

Jeremy Lin

Michael Jordan changed so much in basketball, he took his power to make a difference. It's so much going on in music right now and somebody has to make a difference.

Kanye West

Every memory I had growing up was involving a
basketball. I didn't go to the prom and stuff like that. It was
always basketball for me.

Kevin Durant

When it gets down to it, basketball is basketball.

Larry Bird

The Black Mamba collection of watches is me: It is my
alter ego, so to speak. As I mentioned before, it is sharp,
cutting edge and sleek which are characteristics I try to
apply when I'm out there on the basketball court.

Kobe Bryant

If I weren't earning $3 million a year to dunk a basketball,
most people on the street would run in the other direction if
they saw me coming.

Charles Barkley

You know, I think more people should watch women's basketball. It'd do so much for the game.

Kevin Durant

When people ask me what I miss most about the game, it's being in the locker room and getting to know the guys. Back in those days, we had roommates. We had to talk basketball and that was a great way to understand the game itself and form those lasting relationships.

Earl Monroe

I tell kids to pursue their basketball dreams, but I tell them to not let that be their only dream.

Kareem Abdul-Jabbar

I never gave up as a player, and I won't give up as someone who wants to go to the Hall of Fame, because it's the ultimate goal for a baseball player or a football player or a basketball player.

Pete Rose

That's what I do now: I lead and I teach. If we win basketball games from doing that, then that's great, but I lead and teach. Those are the two things I concentrate on.

Mike Krzyzewski

As I've said, basketball has been, I think, a real cooperative venture. There have been a lot of people that have been involved in it: coaches, administrators - not recently - fans and nobody, nobody any more so than students over the years.

Bobby Knight

You have to be wired a certain way to be a professional basketball player, and the way my body grew, something happened genetically that allowed me to become a lot more explosive.

Jeremy Lin

My life had no meaning at all. I found only brief interludes of satisfaction. It was like my whole life had been about my whole basketball career.

Pete Maravich

When I lose the sense of motivation and the sense to prove something as a basketball player, it's time for me to move away from the game.

Michael Jordan

I also tell them that your education can take you way farther than a football, baseball, track, or basketball will - that's just the bottom line.

Bo Jackson

I've got five grandkids. They play baseball, they play football, they play basketball. I go to all the games. You always have that urge to say something when you're watching them. But I've learned to keep it to myself. I've blurted out some things and embarrassed myself.

John Madden

If all I'm remembered for is being a good basketball player, then I've done a bad job with the rest of my life.

Isaiah Thomas

Basketball is one of those rare opportunities where you can

make a difference, not only for yourself, but for other people as well.

Bill Walton

I am more than just a serious basketball fan. I am a life-long addict. I was addicted from birth, in fact, because I was born in Kentucky and I learned, early on, that Habitual Domination was a natural way of life.

Hunter S. Thompson

If you're playing basketball with someone who's better than you, you have to get better or else it's no fun.

Jason Behr

I was not athletically inclined. I was very quiet, introverted, non-confrontational. My three older brothers were athletes - basketball, football - but I was kind of a momma's boy. Then one day, my brother Roger encouraged me to go to the boxing gym with him. I tried the gloves on, and it just felt so natural.

Sugar Ray Leonard

Basketball is a simple game. Your goal is penetration, get the ball close to the basket, and there are three ways to do that. Pass, dribble and offensive rebound.

Phil Jackson

I was actually supposed to be a basketball player, not an actress. My parents had me playing basketball on competitive teams when I was in kindergarten. Even though my heart belongs to the arts, I'm a tomboy at heart, too.

Zendaya

I have warned many times about the guaranteed dangers of betting with your heart instead of your head - big darkness, soon come - but every once in a while you get a fair chance to have it both ways, and the annual NCAA basketball Tournament is one of them.

Hunter S. Thompson

I wanted to be a football player. Football is a sport that I love, but the more I started playing basketball, the more I started dreaming of playing in the NBA.

Dwyane Wade

I gave everything I had to basketball. The passion is still there, but the desire to play is not. It was a great ride.

Allen Iverson

I lived to play basketball. Growing up as a kid, Bill Russell and the Boston Celtics were my favorite team. The way they played, the teamwork, the sacrifice, the commitment, the joy, the camaraderie, the relationship with the fans.

Bill Walton

Yeah, I like cars and basketball. But you know what I like more? Bananas.

Frankie Muniz

Basketball is like war in that offensive weapons are developed first, and it always takes a while for the defense to catch up.

Red Auerbach

My father made me who I am. He gave me a basketball and told me to play with the ball, sleep with the ball, dream

with the ball. Just don't take it to school. I used it as a
pillow, and it never gave me a stiff neck.

Shaquille O'Neal

I don't have much of an attention span for TV - I nod off
during the basketball playoffs - but when I watch 'Game of
Thrones' on On Demand, I'm glued to the set. It's mystical
and addictive. Tyrion Lannister, that's my man.

Steve Harvey

And I want to do it the right way, like everybody else, not
just a famous figurehead that gets a job because he is a
famous basketball player. I want to really learn the
business.

Shaquille O'Neal

First impressions matter more in basketball than in any
other sport, and they can be savored only in person. Players
can't hide behind pads or helmets, so we can stare at them,
evaluate every move they make: running, jumping,
walking, even ogling the cheerleaders. We can see every
ripple and tattoo. If they're lazy, we can tell.

Bill Simmons

I still regret that I never played soccer in high school. I chose basketball over soccer.

Will Ferrell

I like women's basketball.

Kevin Durant

Until my senior year, baseball and basketball were my best sports; and even when I was a senior, I still wanted to play baseball professionally. But the family wanted me to go to college, and I guess I agreed with them, or else I would have accepted some of the offers I got.

Joe Namath

A friend of mine has a house with a basketball court and a pool. The guys go over and play basketball; I lie by the pool and nap in the sun. That defines me. That's consistent with who I am. I don't pretend to play basketball because I wanna feel like one of the guys. I wanna lie in the sun and relax.

Ryan Seacrest

You can play pickup basketball, but you can't really re-create football.

Peyton Manning

I am, first of all, a basketball player. I've done this for so very long... For me, it's been essential to be successful on the court.

Tony Parker

You know, I'm just 6'9" and 260. And just so happen to be very good at playing the game of basketball.

LeBron James

I won at every level - all the way since I started playing the game of basketball at nine. I've won at every level, won championships at every level. And, you know, it won't be fulfilled until I win at the highest level.

LeBron James

I think as men begin to see things that address them, they will feel that they can relate. They can't relate to 'Basketball

Wives,' 'Housewives of Atlanta.' I am not judging or criticizing those shows at all; what I am saying is the perspective is not necessarily the male perspective. 'Iyanla: Fix My Life' is inclusive of everyone.

Iyanla Vanzant

Kobe Bryant is my favorite basketball player. He takes risks. He goes for the shot. He isn't cautious with whatever he does.

Haley Joel Osment

I think it's important I stay connected to every part of my personality. I play basketball. I rock climb. I paint. I'm a little bit scattered, but it's so I can convincingly play all these characters.

Ansel Elgort

I'm not comfortable being preachy, but more people need to start spending as much time in the library as they do on the basketball court.

Kareem Abdul-Jabbar

I always dreamt of being a basketball player. A dream that only I believed in.

David Duchovny

I played basketball and soccer my freshman year in high school.

Mia Hamm

Few would deny that blacks have become very dominant in athletics: football, basketball, track, now dominant in tennis and dominant in golf.

Jesse Jackson

If you're a basketball player and you don't stop and take pictures with your fans, you can have an amazing game and everyone still loves you.

Kim Kardashian

I think I started learning lessons about being a good person long before I ever knew what basketball was. And that starts in the home, it starts with the parental influence.

Julius Erving

I always wanted to be a basketball player.

Ronnie James Dio

I believe that whatever we have, regardless of a trade being done or not, I feel we have a shot. I've just got to believe that we're going to be all right. I've got to just play basketball.

Allen Iverson

I wanted to be a hockey player. Where I grew up, the basketball courts were rarely used. I was terrible in school and actually said, 'I'm going to be a hockey player.'

Denis Leary

I didn't start sweating until I had children. That was one of the first things I realized when my daughter Violet was born - I started getting wicked BO. You know there's a difference between basketball BO and stress BO? This was definitely stress BO. Like, new dad BO.

Dave Grohl

In sixth grade, my basketball team made it to the league championships. In double overtime, with three seconds left, I rebounded the ball and passed it - to the wrong team! They scored at the buzzer and we lost the game. To this day, I still have nightmares!

Zac Efron

I play basketball all the time. Me and my band play every week on the road. That's something that I've never really given up since high school.

Josh Turner

You don't have to be Wilt Chamberlain to get into the Basketball Hall of Fame. If you don't have a sweet turnaround jumper from 18 feet, the best route to the Hall is fatherhood. Daniel Biasone, aka the 'father of the 24-second clock,' made the cut.

Brendan I. Koerner

I'm a better and more educated person because of basketball.

Lisa Leslie

Playing in the playoffs is the best basketball in the world, and if you can learn under that pressure, succeed under that pressure, it gives you more confidence the next year.

Tony Parker

As a kid, I always idolized entrepreneurs. I thought they were cool people in the way that I thought basketball players were cool people. It's cool that some people get paid to dunk basketballs, but I'm not one of those people.

Ben Silbermann

I like sports, and I enjoy playing basketball and lifting weights.

Joel Osteen

So like any football or basketball coach, you always always believe you're going to win.

Colin Powell

If we can take young people who excel at the highest levels, put them on the same kind of pedestal as the all-state basketball player and the all-state football player, and begin to get the same kind of recognition, it will have a profound effect, and we are finding that it does.

Benjamin Carson

Walking has been ridiculous in college basketball the past 15 years.

Bobby Knight

I pray if I ever find out I have only about three minutes to live it's during a basketball game, because then I'll have, what, 10, 12 years to live?

Elayne Boosler

If this acting thing doesn't work, I'd just put in my resume for NBA.com. I'm a really huge basketball fan... I'll talk all sorts of trash.

Genesis Rodriguez

A lot of times I blend in a little bit easier because I'm not like a basketball player who's going to stand out because of his height.

Tiger Woods

See, my hope and dream is that people have a good time watching basketball. It's not church. It's not serious.

Charles Barkley

Magic is crazy. He is that crazy wild guy on the basketball court that is very intense and very serious. He is the guy who lives and eats and breathes basketball.

Magic Johnson

I like college football, but I'm a huge college basketball fan. I could sit and watch every game of March Madness and be happy. That could be a vacation.

Lewis Black

I have been coaching recently. I coached high school basketball in Arizona, and I hope that more opportunities become available.

Kareem Abdul-Jabbar

It ain't like we're curing cancer or anything, we're watching basketball.

Charles Barkley

With me and basketball, it became part of me.

Mike Krzyzewski

I don't know a lot of show runners. I mean I met a lot of them in picket lines. I'm not part of a, like, secret society or pickup basketball game. As far as I'm concerned, pick-up basketball games are secret societies. They confuse me. I've never been a networker or I've never been very social.

Joss Whedon

I can't palm a basketball.

Carmelo Anthony

Magic Johnson, former basketball player, may run for mayor of L.A. in the next election. Remember the good 'ol days when only qualified people ran for office like actors and professional wrestlers.

Jay Leno

I think probably one of the coolest things was when I went to play basketball at Rucker Park in Harlem. First of all, who would think that Larry the Cable Guy would go to Harlem to play basketball? And I was received like a rock star. It was amazing! There were people everywhere. There were guys walking by yelling, 'Git 'r done!'

Larry the Cable Guy

On an awards-show day, I can play basketball, go in, take a shower and put on a tux - it takes me three minutes to put on a tux - and be out the door in 15 minutes.

George Clooney

I've decided to listen to my doctors and get the procedure I need on my knee. USA Basketball said I had to do what was best for me. They want me to be obviously as healthy as possible so I can continue to play this game at a high level.

Dwyane Wade

For 'Iron Man' I had to improv with Robert Downey Jr., which is like going up against LeBron in basketball. At one point he stopped and said, 'Can we give a round of applause to Olivia, because she's rocking it right now.'

Olivia Munn

My father was a soccer player. All my friends played basketball though, so I stuck with basketball.

Steve Nash

You know I was a shy guy and people didn't know that and still don't know it today. I'm sure basketball brought my shyness out because of the fact that you have to do interviews, and that people are always talking to you in terms of the fans and everything.

Magic Johnson

I tried golf for a while, but I wasn't very good at it, so I didn't play a lot of golf. I enjoy all sports, not just football. I like basketball, baseball, and I got into the World Cup. So really, sports in general are my life, and football specifically.

John Madden

Someday I might have to put down a basketball and have a regular 9-to-5 like everybody else.

Shaquille O'Neal

Michael Jordan was a tremendous basketball player.

Lee Trevino

I'm the basketball version of a gravedigger.

Dennis Rodman

I wanted a NBA basketball gym at my house and that's what I worked hard for and I was able to achieve that.

Terrell Owens

My fondest memories were watching the Beastie Boys get prepped to come on stage. They had a lot of antics and they play a lot of basketball... then they were giving out cameras to the crowd, and performing from the bleachers. The most important thing I learned was that you control your crowd, not the other way around.

Talib Kweli

There's so much that I want to do. I feel like I'm the Magic

Johnson of rap. You know, Magic was great on the basketball court, but he's bigger as a businessman.

Snoop Dogg

I collect different game hats, like Syracuse Women's Volleyball; I have a Navy Basketball hat. They're all vintage but in new condition.

Theophilus London

The tradition in Serbia has always been team sports - football, basketball, handball, volleyball and water polo, individual sports are not supported.

Novak Djokovic

I get scared of a lot of attention. I get scared of the spotlight. And I'm not talking about on the basketball court.

Jeremy Lin

Playing basketball is definitely one of my favorite things to do.

Common

When you're picking a basketball team, you'll take the brother over the guy with the yarmulke. Why? Because you're playing the odds.

Adam Carolla

There's a lot of chatter in basketball and, rightfully, you want players to be talking to each other... But sometimes in practice, it gets too verbose... so I tried to take things out of the ordinary and make them special so they'd understand the difference.

Phil Jackson

I played sports year around: basketball, soccer, softball and I ran track year around, from the time I was, like, six, seven.

Gabrielle Union

Basketball isn't as popular in Canada as it is in the US. Hockey is by far the most popular sport in Canada.

Steve Nash

I play basketball probably four to five days a week when I'm back home.

Josh Hutcherson

In football, there were drinks available everywhere you looked. On a golf tournament, you could find one free anywhere you wanted it. In tennis and NBA basketball, everybody had a hospitality suite, and so you could go there and load up if you wanted to.

Pat Summerall

I love football. My weekends are booked. Saturday college games and Sunday NFL and 'Monday Night Football.' Booked! Football is first, then basketball and then everything else.

Jordin Sparks

I played softball and basketball growing up. I really wanted to play football but both parents said no. I was mad for a second, then got over it. Now, just because I'm tall doesn't mean I can play basketball. I was waaaaay better at swinging a bat.

Jordin Sparks

In high school I was on the basketball team, but the coach did something I didn't dig and the next day he looked up and saw me practising with the football team.

Charles Mingus

Baseball is a slow, boring, complex, cerebral game that doesn't lend itself to histrionics. You 'take in' a baseball game, something odd to say about a football or basketball game, with the clock running and the bodies flying.

Charles Krauthammer

I went to the University of San Francisco on an athletic scholarship. I didn't study in high school. I was just there to get by and to play basketball. But a funny thing happened to me when I got to college. I got challenged by the work and the professors.

Michael Franti

When I'm in Miami I like to go and watch basketball, the Miami Heat.

Andy Murray

I love various sports, including basketball, tennis and billiards.

Yani Tseng

When I look at the system here and look at my position - not just as a basketball player, but when I look around me at the values of the people and the culture and compare them with the values of where I came from - I feel so blessed to be from Africa.

Hakeem Olajuwon

So you're dealing with a coach, and you're dealing with a guy who's actually experienced NBA basketball from a player's perspective and actually goes about it that way.

Kevin Garnett

Every little kid that steps on the court or the field has aspirations to go pro. I think being a pro basketball player is the best job. The thing I had to realize was that I can't do every dream that I have.

Brian McKnight

I can play basketball, run track, and play volleyball, so yeah, I've always been an athlete at heart.

Vivica A. Fox

I try to never lose sight of what a special time it is to be a women's basketball player.

Sue Wicks

It was okay for Wayne Gretzky's dad, for instance, to give him a hockey stick, or Joe Montana's dad to give him a football, or Larry Bird's dad to give him a basketball, but it wasn't okay for Gloria Connors to give her son a tennis racquet.

Jimmy Connors

Celebration is big for me. From my younger days, when I used to win mementos while playing basketball, I have always believed in sharing my success. It has to be there. It lifts the energy levels of the entire side if you are positive and vocal when a wicket falls.

Suresh Raina

I realize that although I'd like to make films as a career after I'm done playing, I really love basketball; I really love my career, an opportunity to compete every day and to push myself physically, mentally and emotionally.

Steve Nash

I coach my daughter's softball and basketball team. We go to all the school functions. We go out to eat at night and take the kids to the movies. We try to be as normal as we can.

Tim McGraw

My dad was the one who really loved basketball, and he was the one that put the basketball in my hands, and my mom was 'Team Mom' of all my teams. I used to play for three or four teams at once and she would just spend her entire afternoon driving me from practice to practice to practice.

Jeremy Lin

One reason outfielders don't have stronger arms might be they don't practice as much as we did. Most teams today don't take outfield practice. Another reason is baseball has to compete with other sports now - basketball, football, soccer - for the better athletes that might have more skills and stronger arms.

Al Kaline

I can score the basketball, but I think I can pass pretty well or I can make the correct pass. I'm not the type of guy who's just going to throw the ball inbounds to a guy who's wide open. I can make the right pass.

Kevin Durant

In my era, where I'm from, I only had Donald Whiteside. He's from Englewood and he's the only one that came out of Englewood. Other than him, I really didn't have anyone else to look up to that was from my area. So in seeing him, I never gave up hope, just kept playing and then I realized that I might have a future in basketball.

Derrick Rose

My sporting hero was Drazen Petrovic, the NBA basketball player, who was killed in a car accident in 1993. He was a good friend, an unbelievable player, and I dedicated my Wimbledon win to him.

Goran Ivanisevic

And it blew my mind when I started to get wind of the fact that they actually liked me being around. That was humbling, because Kentucky basketball is a big deal, and I am not the biggest fan - I am just the most notorious one.

Ashley Judd

True basketball coaches are great teachers and you do not humiliate, you do not physically go after, you do not push or shove, you do not berate, if you are a true coach. If you humiliate or curse them, that won't do it. Coaches like that are not coaches.

Morgan Wootten

Being named as a finalist for the USA Basketball National Team is an unbelievable feeling and an opportunity that is truly humbling. It is an honor to be included with such talented players and I look forward to the chance to represent my country this summer.

James Harden

If you don't like basketball and you're from Kentucky, they'll kick you out!

Josh Hopkins

But the point of using the number was to show that sex was a great part of my life as basketball was a great part of my life. That's the reason why I was single.

Wilt Chamberlain

Basketball talent is basketball talent, no matter if it comes from the suburbs or the city. Take the time to know and understand me before you judge me. Only God can do that. Roses do grow from concrete!

Chris Webber

My mom is real passionate and a family-first woman. She always told me that just because I can shoot a basketball better than someone else, I shouldn't think that I'm better than them. I know if I change, my friends and family would lay me down. She just wants to see her kids do right.

Derrick Rose

Fatherhood will put a man through a lot, but it's a tremendous job, the best in the world - even better than playing basketball.

Derek Fisher

There have been players with Indian heritage, but there hasn't been a Native-American professional basketball player who became a regular for all sorts of social and political reasons.

Sherman Alexie

Free agency screws everybody's allegiances up. Whether it be football, baseball, hockey, basketball, whatever it may be. It's really hard.

Bill Goldberg

I tried out for my basketball team every year and I never made it. You had to buy the shoes before you knew if you were on the team because it took a few weeks for them to ship. I bought the shoes every year, never once made the team, had a ton of high school basketball shoes.

Adam DeVine

Hey, I'm just looking for an excuse to retire so I can play summer league baseball, go coach my nephews, play pickup basketball. I've always had that ability to move on to the next thing.

Doug Flutie

My type of basketball is about how to create space, how to maneuver, how to get your shot off.

Hakeem Olajuwon

Music was definitely a way out. Instead of playing basketball, I was going to recording studios.

Flo Rida

I am reaching a point in my life where the basketball chapter in my life is slowly closing from a competition standpoint.

Alonzo Mourning

I've accomplished everything a person can accomplish on a basketball court, but I never thought about the future when I was younger. I never made plans for the next stage in my life.

Sheryl Swoopes

I was sporty in high school. I played tennis and hockey, and was basketball captain. Then I went to university and stopped doing sport and started eating ice cream.

Rebel Wilson

After spending more than 17 years playing for the NBA, in the summertime, I always came back to community service and different basketball clinics.

Dikembe Mutombo

I used to play soccer when I was in Morocco, but I was more of a basketball player. I played high school basketball, I played AAU basketball.

French Montana

I play basketball to win a championship. That championship is everything to me. And that's what gets people to buy in to your brand - being a winner.

Chris Paul

The cast gets along pretty well, it's a good work

environment. I hang out a lot with Brett Claywell, he plays Tim Smith on the show. We play plenty of basketball.

James Lafferty

I'm 6-foot-4. If my life depended on it, I could still dunk a basketball. Then I would need assistance from a first responder to get down from the rim.

Willie Geist

Whatever I lack in size and strength and speed, I kind of make up for in being grittier. When it comes to something like basketball I'm definitely not the best guy on the court, but I love elbowing and pushing people out or boxing them out.

Steven Yeun

When you think about what the odds are to have four boys to not only be able to follow in the footsteps in a basketball career but to also be good in the secondary career as far as the broadcasting, it's pretty remarkable.

Rick Barry

Basketball Without Borders is a leadership camp that takes basketball to different places around the world, to Africa, Europe, America and Asia. It's a camp that brings players from different parts of the continent to one city that's been assigned as the host city. We've been going to a different city every year.

Dikembe Mutombo

Whirlyball is only the most awesome sport on the planet! It's like bumper cars plus lacrosse meets basketball.

St. Vincent

My goals have gone from being an all-star to just being able to play basketball. I always took for granted that I could play. Now I know what a gift it is.

Rebecca Lobo

By analogy, if we were to develop a soccer team, then we would not invite basketball and volleyball players to the try outs. We would invite soccer players to apply.

Jean-Marie Le Pen

I used to play basketball and I was pretty competitive, but I was never a bad loser. I never got angry. For me it was always about doing my best and devoting myself to a challenge.

Benicio Del Toro

My childhood dream was to play basketball, actually.

Godfrey Gao

My mother used to say, 'You gotta exercise.' She would really pound on me to exercise every day. She was very physically fit; she was on the basketball team in high school in St. Louis in the 1920s, when women didn't do that. And she taught me to play tennis, taught me to walk and run, and I ran for 30 years pretty religiously.

Dick Gephardt

My whole career has been trying to please people in basketball. Now it's time to please myself.

Candace Parker

After I made it to the NBA, I said that I didn't want to be

the last player from Africa. After my rookie year, I went to the league and talked about this, and they embraced my idea and started conducting basketball clinics in Africa, and that's when I knew I wouldn't be the last African.

Dikembe Mutombo

I've always had a passion for giving back. It's a family tradition that comes from my devout parents. They were always giving back and serving the community. So when I became fortunate enough and blessed to play the game of basketball, I was also fortunate enough to follow in my parents' footsteps and give back like the way they did.

Dikembe Mutombo

We look for opportunities to play together including basketball, tennis, swimming, riding bikes and touch football. I try to provide a loving environment where we can play. I think that's good on so many levels - emotionally, for family interactions and, of course, physically.

Alan Thicke

While I sign off on trades or free agents, I've rarely overruled my basketball people's decisions. But I'm not shy about steering the discussion or pushing deeper if something doesn't make sense to me.

Paul Allen

What I know is that if you're going to play half-court, you'd better have the greatest executioners of half-court basketball. If you run, you test the stamina and willpower of the other team. That's what I learned as a player.

Tom Heinsohn

I have a certain taste, and I might be like, 'I like this,' when other people are like, 'I can't wear that.' And in basketball, I might be able to do things other guys might not.

Russell Westbrook

Charles and I go back since college. None of us thought this would happen, we just wanted to play basketball. This is the highest honor that can ever be paid, and it's mind-blowing.

Dominique Wilkins

The game of basketball is one thing, but the image of the game is another thing.

Earl Monroe

I have zero hand-eye coordination - zero - so I've never been good at softball, basketball, golf, things like that, but I'm really strong and I have really good endurance so I can go forever - I'm a tough girl.

Brooklyn Decker

It wasn't about the X's and the O's and the strategy; it was more about keeping 12 guys focused and committed to a task. That group dynamic, and then helping them to grow as people and basketball players.

Isaiah Thomas

Obama's the one who never worked a day in his life. He never earned a penny that wasn't public money. How many fund-raisers does he attend every week? How often does he play basketball and golf? I wish I had that kind of time.

Roger Ailes

I never knew what basketball was. I started playing on the playground. People used to laugh at me and joke at me because I was so tall and I didn't know the game and couldn't play it.

Patrick Ewing

The young Obama's lack of playing time on the high school basketball team was due more to his ability than the coach's preference for white players.

David Moranis

Sure, I like to win when I play basketball or board games or video games, but my day isn't ruined if I lose. I'm always up for a rematch. In all seriousness, that's something that's nice about maturing.

Aaron Staton

I'm someone who always comes on the court no matter what's going on in my life. It's all about basketball and my teammates and my team. I don't let any distractions in, and I bring my best every night, regardless of what's going on or what people are talking about.

Kris Humphries

My dad was always taking photos of us at home, and even

on set - he'd bring us along and stick us in the photos in the background. It was almost the beginning of acting for me, like, 'Hey, you go over there and play basketball in the background, and don't even think about the camera.'

Ansel Elgort

I also developed an interest in sports, and played in informal games at a nearby school yard where the neighborhood children met to play touch football, baseball, basketball and occasionally, ice hockey.

Steven Chu

www.ingramcontent.com/pod-product-compliance
Lightning Source LLC
Chambersburg PA
CBHW070704290526
45790CB00001B/444